# *Precious Jewells - A Gift of the Spirit*

By

*Jewell F. Libkie*

authorHOUSE

*1663 LIBERTY DRIVE, SUITE 200*
*BLOOMINGTON, INDIANA 47403*
*(800) 839-8640*
*www.authorhouse.com*

© 2004 Jewell F. Libkie.
All Rights Reserved.

No part of this book may be reproduced, stored in a retrieval system, or transmitted by any means without the written permission of the author.

First published by AuthorHouse 08/25/04

ISBN: 1-4184-7905-5 (e)
ISBN: 1-4184-7904-7 (sc)

Printed in the United States of America
Bloomington, Indiana

This book is printed on acid-free paper.

I would like to dedicate this book to my Aunt Lela Mitchell, a poet for many years and an inspiration to me. Also to my husband Charlie Libkie, whose encouragement and support was always there for me.

And to God to whom I am thankful for this gift.

# TABLE OF CONTENTS

**CHAPTER ONE  POTPOURRI** .................................................................... 1
    THE OLD HOUSE-OUR HOME ........................................................... 2
    WHERE THE CHILDREN ARE ............................................................ 4
    BEAUTIFUL OCTOBER ....................................................................... 6
    FEELING NO PAIN .............................................................................. 8
    LIFE LINES ........................................................................................... 9
    INSURANCE DILEMMA .................................................................... 10
    IT'S TIME ............................................................................................ 11
    WHO WILL CRY FOR ME? ............................................................... 12
    MY LAST MOVE ................................................................................ 13
    LITTLE BALLERINA ......................................................................... 14
    JUNE DAYS ........................................................................................ 15
    BLESSED WOMAN ............................................................................ 16
    MY WISH FOR Y0U .......................................................................... 17
    PRIORITY ........................................................................................... 18
    WASHING DISHES ............................................................................ 19
    THINGS I LOVE ................................................................................. 20
    BOUQUETS OF LOVE ....................................................................... 22
    FAT FREE ............................................................................................ 23
    GOD'S LITTLE ANGELS ................................................................... 25
    MY DREAM ........................................................................................ 27

## CHAPTER TWO  FAMILY .................................................................. 29

    TO A SPECIAL FATHER ............................................................ 30

    FATHER AND SON ................................................................... 31

    DADDY'S HERE ........................................................................ 32

    MAMA'S SONG ........................................................................ 33

    A CHRISTIAN MOTHER ........................................................... 35

    MOTHER'S CALL ..................................................................... 36

    GOODNIGHT GRANNIE .......................................................... 37

    TRADITION OF THE FLOWER ................................................. 38

## CHAPTER THREE  MEMORIES OF YESTERYEAR ......................... 39

    THE OLD SEAR'S CATALOG .................................................. 40

    HOME REMEDIES ................................................................... 42

    TO A COUNTRY DOCTOR ...................................................... 44

    GRANDMA'S KITCHEN .......................................................... 46

    GRANDMA'S APRON ............................................................. 47

    OUR OLD ROCKING CHAIR .................................................. 48

    THE ROAD HOME .................................................................. 49

    GOING BACK HOME ............................................................. 50

## CHAPTER FOUR  ROMANCE ....................................................... 53

    UNREQUITED LOVE ............................................................... 54

    FIFTY YEARS TOGETHER ....................................................... 55

    A MOMENT SHARED ............................................................. 56

## CHAPTER FIVE  THE GOLDEN YEARS ... 57

- THE GOLDEN YEARS ... 58
- THE SO CALLED "GOLDEN YEARS" ... 59
- CONFUSION ... 60
- SEASONS OF LIFE ... 61
- "HUH" ... 62

## CHAPTER SIX  THE HOLIDAYS ... 63

- IN REMEMBRANCE ... 64
- FREEDOM'S BLESSINGS ... 65
- WE THANK THEE ... 66
- A MODERN THANKSGIVING ... 67
- NO ROOM IN THE INN ... 68
- CHRISTMAS REMEMBRANCE ... 69
- HEAVENLY STAR ... 71
- LIGHTS OF CHRISTMAS ... 72
- LET THE BELLS RING ... 73

## CHAPTER SEVEN  JESUS – THE MAN ... 75

- BE PREPARED ... 76
- THE BEAUTIFUL HANDS OF JESUS ... 77
- WHO IS THIS MAN? ... 79
- HE CAME IN LOVE ... 81
- NO GREATER LOVE ... 82
- LITTLE LOST LAMB ... 83

| | |
|---|---|
| THE GOOD SHEPHERD | 84 |
| GOD'S POINTS OF LIGHT | 85 |
| GIFTS OF LIGHT | 86 |
| PRAYERS AND THANKSGIVING | 87 |
| FRIENDS | 88 |
| **CHAPTER EIGHT THE UNITED STATES OF AMERICA** | **89** |
| AMERICA OUR HOME | 90 |
| WE THE PEOPLE | 91 |
| OUR FLAG | 92 |
| A DAY OF INFAMY | 93 |
| MIRACLE OF GROUND ZERO | 95 |
| **CHAPTER NINE DESERT STORM** | **97** |
| RIBBONS FOR REMEMBRANCE | 98 |
| DESERT STORM | 99 |
| PEACE AFTER THE STORM | 100 |
| WHEELS ACROSS THE DESERT | 101 |

# CHAPTER ONE

## POTPOURRI

# THE OLD HOUSE - OUR HOME

The house had stood by the side of the road
For at least one hundred years.
It was built to shelter families
And keep them safe from fears.

Her walls were strong and true
Her windows gleamed in the sunshine
Her foundations were secure
Letting her soul shine though.

As families moved in, and children came
Their laughter filled the rooms.
Little boys and girls ran and played
They were grown up, and left too soon.

Each family came and went
Leaving their mark in time.
The house was filled with their echoes
Leaving it all behind.

When it was our time to live there
We changed her to suit our style.
We redecorated her inside and out
Again, she seemed to smile.

She saw brides dressing for weddings
And grooms all nervous inside.
She saw grandchildren coming to visit
And also the passing of lives.

The lawn was very beautiful
Trees planted, and flowers grew.
She looked so inviting
Saying welcome to everyone she knew.

Now, here we are in the nineties
She had grown shabby and cold.
No light gleamed from her windows
Again, she was being sold.

All of us who loved her
Remember the days she was "Queen"
When we lived there so happy
She was the American Dream.

Now her walls are tumbled in
I thought I heard her cry.
But as I listened closely
It wasn't her – it was I.

She no longer stands by the side of the road
Progress has taken her place.
But all of us who knew her
Will always remember her grace.

# WHERE THE CHILDREN ARE

I dreamed I went to heaven
And I met an Angel there.
We walked together, and looked around
I saw the Golden Stair.

She showed me the mansions
He went to prepare.
I heard the beautiful singing
No music could compare.

We walked into a beautiful garden
Where the children play.
Oh, they were so happy
All their fears had gone away.

For, these were the abused ones
They suffered so much and died.
Now happy in their new bodies
And they no longer cried.

We walked onto a wonderful place
I stood amazed and felt such love.
There were the millions of babies who died
And now were in Heaven above.

They never had a Mother's love
Their lives were taken away.
So, God called them home, to be with Him
Into a bright new day.

The Angel said, "We heard the cries,
And we saw the terrible pain,"
And Jesus said, "Let them come unto Me,
So they will never hurt again."

And all the little babies
Were gathered unto Him
Where they will dwell forever
Away from this world of sin.

Suddenly, I was awakened
But I felt so warm and loved.
For I had walked with an Angel-
In God's Heaven above.

# BEAUTIFUL OCTOBER

October – the most beautiful time
What beauty to behold.
The sky so blue – the sun so bright
The days are filled with blue and gold.

The nights are filled with stars
The moon is full and bright.
They call it a Hunter's Moon
To light our way at night.

The bright colors of the leaves
The mums are blooming too.
It seems that God has spent the night
Painting it all, for me and you.

The pumpkins are in the field
Golden balls of delight.
The fodder shocks are standing there
Oh, what a beautiful sight.

The apple trees are full of fruit
The limbs are bending low.
Apples shining in the sun
Adds color to the show.

It's harvest time in the land
The bins are full of grain.
Food has been taken from the gardens
God's bounty has come again.

And oh, the smells of Autumn
The air is sweet and clear.
God has washed the earth with rain
Before the frost is here.

I think He made October
Because the time near
When the leaves will be gone
And color will disappear.

We will carry the beauty all Winter
To warm our hearts everyday
In memory, the Blue and Gold of October
Will keep sunshine—along our way.

# FEELING NO PAIN

This little pill has a mystery
How does it know where to go?
How does it know where the pain is?
In you head, or in your toe?

Your head is aching really badly
You take a pill or two.
You have complete faith in them
To know just what to do.

It's very confusing when you go
To buy something for the pain.
Should you buy tablets, capsules, or caplets?
It's a problem that is plain.

And that isn't the only thing
There are so many kinds to buy.
The shelves are loaded with choices
Which one should you try?

There is Anacin, Excedrin, and Motrin
Tylenol is the Doctor's choice.
You read all the labels and wonder
Which one will make you rejoice?

There is one way to find out
Which one works for you?
Take them for a period of time
And see what each one will do.

There is one thing you know for sure
Wherever you have a pain.
Just take two pills and a glass of water
And soon you will feel fine again!

# LIFE LINES

Somewhere in our lives
We have to cross a line.
To take a stand and do what is right
And let our light shine.

God has drawn a line
In this world of pleasure and sin.
We have to be careful and not step across
And destroy us, from within.

Once we go beyond —
Into the pleasures, to feed the Monday then we have drawn a line, between us and God
Because we have left Him behind.

In pleasure, all of our idols
Have feet of clay.
They disappoint us, and make us sad
And our hearts are turned away.

In the arenas — there is violence
It isn't for fun and games, anymore, you know.
The more broken bones and bloodshed
The better we like the show!

There is nothing wrong
With having fun and game.
We need to clean it up
And make them right again.

So now, we need to get back
Over that line — again.
And get our priorities straight
To cleans us from within.

When this live is over,
And our race is finally run
May God say to us at last,
"Well done, my child, well done."

# INSURANCE DILEMMA

Insurance, what a question.
How are we supposed to know?
We read the lines – it's foreign
Just fill in the blanks below.

How can we understand
The language that they use?
Nothing makes any sense
It gives us all the blues.

We, just ordinary people
Need someone to explain
Even then, we don't understand
We feel it is all in vain.

They always manage to pay
Less than we would like
They make it sound so legal
It gives us quiet a fright!

It seems that the outcome
No matter what they say
We always wind up
Paying anyway!

# IT'S TIME

There is a time for everything
It is written for us to see.
There is a plan for each of us
A time for you and me.

There is a time to be born
And there is a time to die.
That's the beginning and the ending of our life
And we often wonder why.

There is a time to plant
And soon the harvest comes.
That is a time to reap
God's blessing, one by one.

There is a time to laugh
And we are happy and we play.
Our hearts are full of joy
And we dance our cares away.

Sometimes our hearts are filled with music
We hear the beauty it brings.
We love to sing the great songs
Until it is time for other things.

There is a time for sadness
And tears fill our eyes.
It's a time of heartbreak
That nearly costs our lives.

So take the time for worship
Take time to laugh and sing.
Sow and reap, work through the day
And you will find time for everything.

But no matter what time it is
From the beginning to the end
God's love will always be there
We have no better friend.

# WHO WILL CRY FOR ME?

In this life many tears are shed
For many different things.
We cry for joy, sorrow and pain
And other things, our life may bring.

Tears come, to see a bride
All dressed up in gleaming white.
The groom all nervous, waiting with love
For her to become his wife.

When we see a newborn baby
Coming into this life
The mother holding it, with so much love
And the father adoring his wife.

I look around and see the ones
Who have lived for so many years.
The faltering footsteps, the body frail
It fills our eyes with tears.

We weep when we see the loved ones
Of a soldier brave and true
Given the carefully folded flag
Because he dies for me and you.

It seems, I am always in tears
Filling my eyes until I cannot see.
And then, I wonder to myself
Will anyone weep for me?

And then I remember with a smile
How blessed I have always been.
With loved ones all around me
They weep for me now and then.

Now I understand — we share
In each other's life, you see.
As I cry for those I love,
They will be crying for me.

# MY LAST MOVE

Everyone loves to move
Into a brand new home.
All new, clean and beautiful
Never again to roam.

They make lots of preparations
Getting ready for the big event.
Buying everything brand new
It's really money well spent.

I have moved many times
Sometimes far away.
But always there was preparation
Getting ready for the moving day.

Someday, I will move again
This time into a mansion made for me.
And I can't wait to go there
It will be my last move, you see.

Jesus promised us a place
That he would go to prepare.
It's ready and waiting for me
It's so wonderful there.

We will live next door to Angels
And we will walk in heavenly light.
We can sit down and talk with Jesus
Anytime of the day or night.

We will walk on streets of pure gold
We will hear the angels sing
There will be a Heavenly choir
And Jesus will be King!

So, I'm making preparations
Won't you come along and see
The mansion in Heaven
That was prepared for Me?

# LITTLE BALLERINA

Dance, little ballerina, dance
Hear the music play.
You in your tutu, and ballet shoes
Dance the day away.

You look so beautiful
Your hair shining under the lights.
On your toes, spinning and dancing
You are a beautiful sight!

You are as graceful as can be
Spinning and leaping into the air.
You hear the music playing
It carries you — here and there.

So dance little ballerina.
Thrill us and spin away
On your toes, you are twirling
You will dance night and day.

So dance away to Dreamland
On a pink cloud — you will play.
Your twinkling toes will take you
To Ballerina Land far away ......

# *JUNE DAYS*

June is the month of love
Of brides and grooms and rings.
It's moonlight by night and sun by day
And roses and shady lanes.

It's strawberry time—oh so good.
Soft breezes and butterfly wings
And humming birds hovering over flowers
And many other things.

It's honeymoon time for newlyweds.
Oh, how they cherish these June days.
Also for Silver and Golden Anniversaries
And children happy at play.

June is the time, when the year is half gone.
We store up memories, for days to come
They will warm our hearts all winter
Remembering our time in the sun.

Those beautiful days of sunshine
Of blue skies and happy faces.
And white fluffy clouds floating by
To other June day places.

# BLESSED WOMAN

I went to church this morning
And found my way to a seat.
There beside me sat a lady
Dressed so nice and neat.

We greeted each other with a smile
Her eyes still had a twinkle.
Her hair was beautiful silver gray.
Her face was lined with wrinkles.

She was so happy to be there
To worship with her friends.
She listened to the music
Her voice blending right in.

When we stood up for prayer
She could hardly rise and stand.
She bowed her head, and closed her eyes
And folded her work worn hands.

I looked down at those hands
And thought of all they had done.
A long life of service
Working, and helping everyone.

She listened to the preacher
Sometimes a soft "Amen".
And when we stood to be dismissed
As the service came to an end,

I watched her as she left the church
She smiled and walked away.
I knew that she was happy
Because God blessed her on that day.

# MY WISH FOR YOU

If I could have the power
On this our special day.
I'd change the world for all of you
With peace and love to stay.

There would be no wars anywhere
The planes and ships would travel for fun.
I'd chase all the shadows
And fill your life with sun.

I'd make every hour a happy one
With your loved ones always near.
There would always be smiles
And never a frown or a tear.

Now, we both know that can't be
Life just isn't that way.
We have both sunshine and shadows
That fill up every day.

So, all I can do is say a prayer
That God will carry you
Across the times of worry
And shorten them for you.

So my wish is as always
That in a special way
God will bless you richly
And He will be with you every day.

# *PRIORITY*

There is a box within our home
It's called a television set.
We plan our lives around it
Nothing has stopped it yet!

We have lost the art of talking
And singing while we work.
We don't even read the paper
Or read our favorite book.

Neighbors have stopped calling
Afraid they will interfere.
With soap operas and game shows
And other shows so dear.

Our holidays and weekends are taken
With sports that dominate our lives.
It's caused trouble between family members
And some of them won't survive.

But now, it's time for vacation
It's here just in time you see.
The family is finally together again
And happy as they can be.

And here we are at a motel
To stop for a good night's rest.
So what is the first thing we do?
Why, its turn on the old T.V. set!

# *WASHING DISHES*

When I was a little girl
Washing dishes was my chore.
I never liked to do them
There was nothing I hated more.

Sticky glasses and greasy plates
Not to mention the pots and pans.
That old black skillet was the worst
It absolutely ruined my hands.

I always put it off
As long as I could get by.
Sooner or later, I had to go
I would attack them with a sigh.

Now I have a home of my own
Many years have passed.
I have washed dishes all my life
But I have found peace at last.

Now in this world today
People are starving everywhere.
There are homeless people in the streets
So many cupboards are bare.

Now when I see my table
Dirty dishes ready to be done
I realize how lucky I am
That they are there and I won't run.

Because they mean we are blessed
There was food that we ate.
We were nourished and fed
By the bounty on our plate.

So, I fill the sink with hot water
And it's soapy bubbles rise,
A song fills my heart and I thank God
Because He is the one who supplies.

# THINGS I LOVE

There are some things I love
It seems they never change.
Little things I remember
Let me try to explain.

I love to smell the new mown grass
On a warm June day.
And smell the fresh cut flowers
To make a summer bouquet.

I love to see a lovely bride
As she walks slowly down the aisle.
Her father walking proudly
And the groom begins to smile.

I love to see a baby
All rosy and warm from a nap.
How sweet they are and loving
When you take them on your lap.

I love a patch of violets
As they bloom in the spring.
And those wonderful mushrooms
Just after a soft falling rain.

I love to see "Old Glory"
Waving against a clear blue sky.
She stands for freedom in our land
We feel so proud as we go by.

And oh, that smell of coffee
As it perks at the break of day.
With bacon frying in the pan
We are ready to face the day.

I love my family around me
Ones I hold so dear.
My husband standing by my side
I'm safe I feel no fear.

And now, I feel so blessed
As I thank my Father above
That He has given me all of these
Little think I love.

# BOUQUETS OF LOVE

In my live, I have received
Many bouquets of flowers
Corsages, planters and vases
That gave me happy hours.

Usually they were give in love
By someone who really cared.
Each one was so precious
Each was a moment shared.

Sometimes they came from a sweetheart
A corsage to wear over my heart.
Sometimes from a very good friend
Who would someday have to depart.

But the flowers, I never will forget
Usually daisies in a sweaty little hand
Was brought to me on a sunny day
There was none finer, in all the land.

Now, the flowers live in my memory
The little ones have all gone away.
They have grown up and departed
But they are in my heart to stay.

Now, when I see a field of daisies
On a bright sunny day in May
I picture them in a clean jelly glass
And remember how they brightened my day.

# *FAT FREE*

We are glad to live in a country
Where it is the land of the free.
We are so glad to have the three freedoms
And now, we have another, fat free!

We have lived on the fat of the land
And we really have lost control.
And now we have another kind
Fast foods for the body and soul.

We never thought of cholesterol
That's the result of the foods we eat.
We take all kinds of vitamins
And we are going down in defeat.

You walk down the aisle, of the grocery store
And it is written on every food you see.
We read all the labels — one stands out
In big letters it — Fat Free!

It shows up in our bread
And boxes of crackers too.
And cereal that we love so dear
Has gone Fat Free now, for me and you.

We buy a head of lettuce
And find a salad dressing too.
Never fear — it is okay to eat
Because, they are Fat Free too!

Remember in the good old days
When our food was so delicious and good?
Biscuits and sausage gravy, and a piece of pie
Everyone was at the table, when it was served

So now, we listen to our Doctors
Because of blood pressure so high.
We take our pills and go on
And think of Pizza — with a sigh.

It's time to make my dinner
I don't know what it will be.
But one thing for sure and certain
It's going to be — Fat Free!

# GOD'S LITTLE ANGELS

God must have a special place
For all those little souls in his care.
Angels must collect them and take them
Because they will be loved and sheltered there.

God loves the little children
Jesus said, "Let them come unto Me"
As He gathered them around Him
How He loved them, was plain to see.

He said, "If anyone harms one of these, it would be better
For a rock to be around their neck, and cast into the sea;
Whatever you do, to one of these
You also do it — unto Me."

So now, in this world we live in
They are hurt and abused in every way.
Doctors and nurses in hospitals — wipe tears
Because, they see them, beaten and abused every day.

On T.V. and newspapers — are full of news.
About newborns, thrown out and unloved.
The little bodies found in dumpsters and snow banks
But their souls — are taken to Heaven above.

But there are those little ones
Whose lives are snuffed out, without a care.
They never get to live and feel love
Because no one wanted them there.

They were conceived, close to the mother's heart.
God meant them to be, blessing of love.
He made a place, in the mother's body
Where it is nurtured, and kept safe from up above.

So now, we have a beautiful vision
In Heaven's garden, up above.
Where all these precious little souls
Are wrapped in God's Holy Love!

"You must become as little Children, for such is the Kingdom of Heaven."

# MY DREAM

I dreamed I was on my way to Heaven
But I was stopped at the Pearly Gates.
They said, "You can't get inside
Until you pass the test."

An Angel took me by the hand
Where I had to stand in line.
I couldn't see what was ahead
I wondered, what would I find?

I saw some turn away in sorrow
With tears and disbelief.
And some went in, rejoicing
And I felt some relief.

Finally it was my time
A beautiful table was there.
And on it a large Golden Book
That I would soon share.

There sat an Angel, dressed in white
And He opened up the Book
And soon He found my name
He invited me to look.

It seemed to hold some records
Of all my deeds — good and bad.
Some of the things written there
Made me very sad.

I saw where I had omitted
To carry out God's will.
It seemed I was too busy
Yes, I remember it well.

After the Angel studied my life
He said, "Your sins have been forgiven
Let's look in the Book of Life
And see if you can enter in."

He said, "If your name is written here
It is the only way —
If you took Jesus, into your heart
And walked with Him everyday."

"Let us see if it is here,
written in the Book of Life"
and as He opened the precious Book
I awoke from my dream that night.

So, it left me wondering
What the answer could be
I seemed to hear Jesus say
"I gave my all for you — what have you given for me?"

# CHAPTER TWO

---

## FAMILY

# TO A SPECIAL FATHER

Today is a very special day
Set aside for one we hold dear.
It's for our earthly Father
Whom we love and revere.

He has always been there when we need him
We rely on his strength and care.
We always used him as our example
His time he is willing to share.

When we meet around our table
His head is always bowed in prayer.
He teaches us to be thankful
For the food that mother prepared.

On Sunday he takes us to worship
He teaches us about God and His love.
He tells us about our Heavenly Father
Who lives up in Heaven above.

We want to walk in Dad's footsteps
We know he will carry us through.
He'll never mislead or misguide us
We can trust him in all that we do

So today tell him you love him
Make his a King for a day.
If he doesn't live near you — call him
And wish him a "Happy Father's Day."

# *FATHER AND SON*

I saw a little boy today
He was walking with his Dad.
Hand in hand they went along
Looking so happy and glad.

Dad was so proud of his little son
Who was trying to keep in stride.
But his little legs were much too short
So Dad carried him instead.

As I walked on — I thought
Of the sweet love they had
And how safe and secure the child felt
In the arms of his loving Dad.

It's very much like that with us
As we live from day to day
How our Heavenly Father loves us
And carries us on our way.

# DADDY'S HERE

We are going to honor Father
Because we love him so.
He has guided us all through life
Showing us the way to go.

He held us when we were babies
In loving arms — we had no fear.
In his hands he cradled us
He would say, "It's alright — Daddy's here".

As children we would stumble
He would lift us up so gentle and dear.
He would wipe our tears away and say,
"It's alright — Daddy's here".

As we grew into our teens
Those were our uncertain years.
We needed a stern hand to guide us
He was there, always saying, "Daddy's Here".

By this time, sometimes we disagreed.
Sometimes we turned away with a sneer.
Later on, things got rough, he came
And we would hear him say, "It's alright — Dad's here".

Now, we have children of our own
And we want them to feel no fear.
I'll always remember my dad and say,
"It's alright, my child, Daddy's here".

It's the same with our Heavenly Father
He is always there, have no fear.
When things go wrong and we feel along
If we listen, we will hear him say,
"It's alright, Your Father is here."

# MAMA'S SONG

When I was just a little girl
Things were so different then.
The thing that entertained us most
Was when my Mama sang.

Our house didn't have the music and noise
From a radio or television set.
The music we had we made ourselves
They weren't invented yet.

My sister and I have our memories.
We thought we were rich in things.
Mama would take us in the big rocking chair
And we listened to the song mama sings.

She knew all kinds of songs
Funny ones, religious and sad.
She sang to us of lost babes in the woods
And we would cry and feel so bad.

She sand the old folk songs
Of lost loves of long ago.
Also, cute little nursery rhymes
To us it was the same as a show.

She did her housework well
Her voice always had a glad ring.
As she cleaned and dusted the house
Always, Mama would sing.

We learned so much from her
She sang when things went wrong.
We saw her spirits lift
When Mama sang her song.

And now she is at home in Heaven
As she is working around God's throne
I know she is so very happy
And she will be singing her song.

And these times we live in now
There is noise and confusion all day long.
When things get hectic and I am tired
I think of Mama, and when she sang a song.

# A CHRISTIAN MOTHER

Mothers are so special
God made them that way.
He needed someone to help Him
Care for the children every day.

When He decided to replenish the earth
He knew there would be children everywhere
Their needs would be so great
They must have special care.

He knew every child would need someone
Every minute of the day.
To be there with unselfish love
To teach them His special way.

So down through all the years
Our wonderful Mothers were there.
She has fed us, loved us, and taught us
Everything in life to share.

Your Mother has loved and cared for you
Putting your needs ahead of her own.
She is the best friend you will ever have
No matter where you may roam.

She is the keeper of the flame
The center of every home.
She nourishes those who live there
Guided by God alone.

Let her know you love her
And in this month of May
Don't forget to honor her
On her special Mother's Day.

# MOTHER'S CALL

When evening shadows lengthen
And twilight beings to fall
It's then my thoughts turn backwards
To a time when we were small.

Just at the time I felt fear
And needing to come home safe
The door would open and in the light
There was Mother, a smile on her face.

"Children, you come in now
It's time to leave your play
Suppers already, its time to eat
Come in now, come right away."

Oh, how good to hear her call
"Children, it's supper time".
My fears all vanished, I ran inside
Leaving those shadows behind.

Oh, just to go back and hear that voice
Calling us in from our play
"Come in children, come now, you hear?
Tomorrow's another day".

Someday she will call us again
We will hear that sweet voice one more
"Come on children, come on in
we will help you safely to shore".

And then I'll be safe and secure
Such love, as we have never known.
I'll be there for supper with Mother
And Jesus, around God's throne.

# GOODNIGHT GRANNIE

When Grannie goes to bed at night
She is a funny sight
She wraps her head in toilet paper
With a net tied on so tight.

It holds the "set" she says
And with that I will agree
Because the next morning
She looks fine to me!

I don't know if she uses Charmin
Or maybe it is Cottonelle
Might have been a brand
That happened to be on sale!

But whatever my Grannie does
It's alright with me
I'll always love her anyway
She is sweet as she can be.

When she wakes up at morning
She is ready for the day
She looks at me and smiles
And hugs the night away.

# TRADITION OF THE FLOWER

When I was a child
We had a tradition for Mother's Day
We always wore a flower to honor her
But in a different way.

If your Mother was still alive
The flowers were warm and bright.
But if she had gone to Heaven
The flowers were the purest white.

Usually if white was worn
It came from the locust tree.
Or sometimes the Lily of the Valley
They grew in you're your, you see.

But when we were luck
And she was with us still
Red was the favorite color to wear
But we used others as well.

There was another tradition,
If you wore the locust alone
You wore the blossoms turned up, if she lives,
And down if she had gone on.

Down through the years a change came
Loved ones bought us corsages to wear.
But I think it is nice to remember
The tradition that started back there.

They say that time changes everything
And that is usually so true
It doesn't matter in what way we do it
That's between your Mother and you.

# CHAPTER THREE

## MEMORIES OF YESTERYEAR

# THE OLD SEAR'S CATALOG

There was one thing when I was a child
That we all held so dear
It was the Sears and Roebuck Catalog
It came twice every year.

We got one in the Spring
And also in the Fall.
They opened up a land of dreams
I sometimes love to recall.

Now we didn't have television
Or even a radio
The only things we got from the world outside
Were the phonograph and the movie show.

But when we got that catalog
Each page brought fantasies untold
We wished for the toys and the beautiful clothes or dreams were like spun gold.

My sister and I would lie on the floor
And look at page after page
We would wish for all those wonderful things
There was something for every age.

Even Mom and Dad had favorite things
They turned to once in awhile
With a far away look in their eyes
And sometimes a little smile.

The Fall and Winter was always the best
Because of the Christmas section there
There were toys and candies and wonderful things
That all children wished they could share.

It truly was a wish book
Better than the television commercials today
We spent many long winter evenings
Just wishing and dreaming away.

Now we have our Shopping Malls
And televisions to show their wares
But, somehow it just doesn't compare
To that wonderful Catalog from Sears!

# HOME REMEDIES

When I was just a little girl
Medication was different then
There weren't all these fancy drug stores
Home remedies weren't invented then.

The doctor didn't write for you
A prescription you could fill
He gave you a few pills
And a liquid that would kill!

But worst of all was Grandma
She relied on Castor Oil
There was no way to get out of this
No one you could call.

My mom greased us with Vicks Salve
Our chest, throat and nose
There wasn't anything it wouldn't cure
It was what she always chose.

That was better than skunk grease
She sometimes applied.
I often thought it would be better
If I could just have died!

I remember there were times
I surely will never forget
A little bag of Asafetida was used
On a string around my neck.

And oh, that terrible enema
How we screamed and cried
Mama was so determined
Again—I would rather have died.

But now, we go to the doctor
We get a shot in the hip or arm
A prescription to fill at the drug store
We may have to mortgage the farm!

There was a secret ingredient they used
As they nursed us with tender loving care
They prayed to our Heavenly Father
He answered, He was always there.

They trusted in Him completely
As they applied these things with love
They knew He watches over us
From his Heavenly Home above.

# TO A COUNTRY DOCTOR

He was a dedicated Country Doctor
He had so much to share
They came to him from miles around
Just to be in his care.

His small office was always crowded
With patients who trusted in him.
He never turned anyone away
And they returned again and again.

He made house calls — day and night
He traveled through rain, sleet and snow
When the call came and he was needed
Out into the night he would go.

He swabbed their throats and gave them pills
And sometimes even a shot.
He did it all with loving care
To be sure they never forgot.

He delivered babies in the home
Sometimes by a coal oil light.
When the labor was hard and long
He would stay and spend the night.

He did the same for the rich and the poor
Sometimes never getting paid at all.
He loved his patients, and went to them
He never missed a call.

Sometimes a farmer would pay him
In produce from their land.
Chickens, eggs, butter and milk.
Or whatever they had on hand.

He carried a black bag everywhere
Full of medicine for all our ills.
Children thought it held babies
As well as bright colored pills.

He had no nurse all dressed in white
No secretary to schedule his time.
Appointments wasn't made — no bills sent out
Those who needed him most we first in line.

He was respected by all the Doctors
In the city and in the Hospital nearby.
They came gladly to aid him
Knowing on him, they could rely.

I am sure in the Bloomington Hospital
Somewhere you can find his name
Dr. George Mitchell he was one of a kind
That will never be seen again.

The Country Doctor of Fifty Years ago!

# GRANDMA'S KITCHEN

I remember Grandma's kitchen
What a wonderful place to be.
It was like a haven from the world
It meant so much to me.

It was the heart of the house
With a wood range, always warm.
Something was always simmering
To be eaten late on.

A long table was there
Where the family met each day.
They gathered around its bounty
And bowed their heads to pray.

The morning hours were spent
Baking and preparing the food.
The pies — for eating pleasure
Sometimes, cookies or cake — oh so good!

Oh, it smelled heavenly
It was swept and cleaned each day.
The sun streamed in the windows
Inviting you to stay.

It was a place where love was shared
Sometimes laughter and tears.
Some one was always there for us
In memory has lasted through the years.

Just to go back again, to that kitchen
But it isn't there anymore.
Grandma's kitchen is in Heaven now
And only God can open the door.

# *GRANDMA'S APRON*

My Grandma wore an apron
She put a clean one on everyday.
She never was without it
All ladies dressed that way.

She wore it in the kitchen
When she was making food.
She went out to the woodpile
And filled it full of wood.

She used that apron for everything
She would fill it full of corn
She would throw it out to the chickens
To feed them in the morn.

She would put the eggs in her apron
As she gathered them from the nests.
She would carry them all the way to the house
And never make a mess.

When children were hurt and came crying
She gathered them up in her arms.
Gently she wiped the tears from their eyes
With that apron—so soft and warm.

She cuddled the babies and rocked them to sleep
With that apron tucked around.
As she held them close—and sang to them
No greater comfort could be found.

I wonder today, as I read in the news.
About our your people running wild
I wonder if there had been someone around
Wearing an apron—to comfort that child!

Would they have turned out different
Wrapped in that cloak of love
With Grandma who wore an apron
Guided by God above.

# OUR OLD ROCKING CHAIR

I loved that old rocking chair
In the living room back home
Where I grew up, within its arms
I never felt alone.

My Mother rocked me gently
When I was needing care.
Sometimes I was ill with a fever
And she was always there.

Sometimes it was the carriage
That carried me away.
In my imagination we traveled
To a different place everyday.

It was in this chair we heard stories
And learned little nursery rhymes.
We heard fold songs of long ago
Of other places and times.

Oh, I wish I had that old chair today
But it has been gone for many years
I will always cherish the memory
As I remember, with smiles and tears.

# THE ROAD HOME

It is said you can't go home again.
But I don't think it's true.
All roads lean home as Festival time
And home is waiting for you.

It's reunion time for everyone
Those who have traveled from far away
To see family and places
They have remembered everyday.

When they come home they will find
That same old spirit is here.
People working together to make a Festival
The best one year after year.

Through laughter and tears together
We will be thinking of those so dear
Who are no longer here to greet you
But you know their spirit is here.

No matter which road you may take
Your cars, vans, buses, and planes
They will all bring you Home — again
And you will see, it's all the same.

You, all roads lead home
To a place you will always remember.
So, come on back to the Fall Festival
And we will be looking for you--
In September!

# GOING BACK HOME

I went to my old hometown
The place I hold so dear.
I looked for all the places
That I loved when I was there.

I saw the house where I was born
The places where I had played.
I saw the yard where my friend and I
Enjoyed its cooling shade.

As I looked around, the place had changed.
I hardly knew the town.
The old school that I loved was gone
And other places could not be found.

I went to see the little church
That stood upon a hill.
But it was even gone by now
But I remember it still.

The old grocery store where we bought our food
Has also gone by the way.
There is no other like it, in all this world
Oh, I wish I could go back today.

That wonderful man that kept the store
He was our dear benefactor and friend.
We still remember his hearty laugh
He knew we had no money to spend.

He saw us eyeing the candy
As he took our orders to fill.
He always gave us some of it
We think of him lovingly still.

Then there was the old Post Office
Where we went everyday for the mail.
You also heard all the news of the day
Friends visited there without fail.

Now, as I stand and look around,
There's one more place to see
The Doctor's little office
It brings a painful memory.

He gave us our shots and swabbed our throats,
He bound up our bleeding knees
He took our temperature and gave us pills
He cared so much for you and me.

Now, it's getting late, but before I go,
There's another dear place, I must see
There it is, my grandparent's home
Where they always welcomed me.

As I look around the town
I think of all these dear people again
For awhile I went back in memory
And everything was the same.

But now as I look again—I see
New places have replaced the old.
I realize I have been walking through memories
In a place that's more precious than gold.

I know we all have a hometown
That in memory we can see it everyday
It will be a part of us forever-
Nothing can ever take it away.

I think that when we leave this world
And gather around God's throne
All those loved ones from our hometowns
Will help us safely home.

# CHAPTER FOUR

## ROMANCE

# *UNREQUITED LOVE*

She was such a little thing
So feminine in every way.
She fell in love completely
Much more than she could say.

He was so tall and handsome
So majestic and so strong.
And when he saw her standing there
His heart filled with a song.

Although they were very much in love
There was a problem from the start.
They only wanted to be together
And never, ever part.

She watched him from her window
As he walked across her yard.
She knew at once it could never be
For she was a Miniature Poodle and he was a St. Bernard!

# *FIFTY YEARS TOGETHER*

We have been married for fifty years.
A day we will never forget.
We promised to love one another
Our vows we always have kept.

We have built our house on the solid rock
That is grounded in Heaven above.
It has held fast through many a storm
And we held onto our sweet love.

We have stood together, through happiness and tears
And trusted God each step of the way.
We have gone through shadows and sunshine
During our life together, day by day.

We wear our Golden wedding rings
A symbol of eternal love.
We remember placing them on our fingers
And were blessed by God above.

We have been through sickness, and good health
There have been hard times to weather.
We have seen our children go off to war
But we always stayed together.

We comforted each other when times were bad.
We shared our sorrows and joys.
We raised a family of which we are proud
Beautiful girls, and fine handsome boys.

To live together for so many years
You have to be loving, honest and true,
Be unselfish live for one another
And consider each other, in all that you do.

# *A MOMENT SHARED*

She was a beautiful little dog
A snow white Poodle so fair.
She lived in a mansion on the hill
Like a Princess — I couldn't share.

I was a mongrel, scrubby and lean
Hungry all the time
No home or family to care for me.
I knew I couldn't cross the line.

The line was a place in town
With the rich upon the hill
Down below across the tracks
The poor worked in the Mill.

One day as I was hunting
For a bite of food somewhere
I looked for a moment toward the hill
And I saw her standing there.

The collar she wore around her neck
Sparkled in the sun
Her black shining eyes invited me
To come and have some fun.

At that moment in time, I fell in love
With never a care in the world
I saw no line between us
My head was in a whirl.

I knew she fell in love with me
Her eyes told me so
She danced around me — so happy
I just couldn't turn and go.

We found a little haven
It was our private place
We learned about each other
As we stood there face to face.

Wait now, here comes her Mistress
With fire in her eye.
I'll have to run back down the hill
Without a real goodbye.

Now, I will always remember
When time stood still
When I shared a glorious moment
With my Princess on the hill.

# CHAPTER FIVE

---

# THE GOLDEN YEARS

# THE GOLDEN YEARS

My wish is for the very best
Everyday in the year
I'm a little behind with this
I'm always bringing up the rear.

It seems I get slower
With each passing day.
I always aim to do it right
But things get in my way.

Sometimes I wonder what to do
My memory fails at times.
I walk around and ask myself
What did I have in mind?

I walk from room to room
And wonder why I'm there
I must be looking for something
But what, I wonder where.

But one thing is for certain
As soon as I sit down to rest
Suddenly, I remember everything
And give it all my best.

I hope you get to read this poem
It depends on whether or not
I finished it up, and typed it out
Or again—if I forgot!

# THE SO CALLED "GOLDEN YEARS"

I've reached the time in my life
They call the "Golden Years"
The way has been hard at times
But now, I'm finally here.

The hardest thing I do all day
Is climb out of bed.
I wash my face, and brush my teeth
And get myself dressed.

I go into the kitchen
The coffee is perking away.
It smells so good — I pour a cup
Maybe, I'm up for the day.

Now if I could just remember
What I'm going to do today
If I can find my glasses
I'll just be on my way.

But I don't need to worry
Because the day I was sixty-five
I got on good old Medicare
To help me keep alive.

Ah, yes, these are the "Golden Years"
There has been fun, laughter and tears
And if I can just get up tomorrow
I'll try for a few more years!

# CONFUSION

I've come to the time in my life
When it seems that I always "forget".
I don't know if I'm coming or going
Sometimes, I do thing, I regret!

Now, I don't know about you
If you have had this happen or not
I'm always trying to remember
All the things, I already forgot.

I walk into the kitchen
And walk up to the sink
Did I come here to wash my hands?
Or did I need a drink?

I walked into the bedroom
Why did I come to this spot?
I didn't bring anything with me
So I came after something — but what?

I try all day to remember
Something that I forgot
Or search for something I misplaces
Whether it is important — or not.

So, I hope you will read my poem
It depends on whether or not
I remembered to write it today
Or whether, again, I forgot!

# SEASONS OF LIFE

In the springtime of life
I'm having a ball.
Working so hard, in the garden and all.
But I will rest — later on you can bet
When the works all done this fall.

In the summer of life
There are tasks great and small.
Besides all the picnics and parties around
Oh, what a whirlwind, no rest to be found
I'll just wait — until the works all done this fall.

Now it's autumn, with leaves blowing in the wind.
The food is all harvested, the grain in the bin
I've had no rest at all.
So come along with me — to sit awhile
For the works all done this fall.

Now it's the wintertime of my life
We are waiting for Jesus to call —
I think I'll be going to meet Him, now
That the works all done, this fall.

# "HUH"

When you are in the Golden Years
They say it's a wonderful time.
The ones who say this
Are living in their prime.

They don't know what goes on
And "goes" is the right word.
Your eyesight, your teeth, your legs, and your hearing
None of them can be cured.

We never believe, that we can't hear
It's because people are mumbling, we say
They aren't saying the words very clear
Seems they are worse everyday.

So finally, we go for a hearing aid
I thought my troubles were done
But little did I know what was in store
If I had, I sure would have been on the run.

Now I hear noises you wouldn't believe
Everything is loud and clear.
I hear everything that's going on
Except what you are saying, my dear!

# CHAPTER SIX

# THE HOLIDAYS

# *IN REMEMBRANCE*

They lie beneath the grass so green
Sleeping, and resting in peace.
They gave their lives for their country
Hoping wars would forever cease.

On Memorial Day, we honor them
They were our Country's best.
They shed their blood on foreign soil
And then were laid to rest.

There are rows and rows of white markers
With their names printed, for all to see
And a loving hand placed a flag there
Because of them, we are still free.

Every little town has a service
Where their names are read one by one.
Tears are shed, and we hear "Taps"
All remembering, a Husband, Daughter or Son.

We hope and pray, peace will come
As our Flag waves over our land
Let freedom ring — within our hearts
And place it all in God's hand.

# *FREEDOM'S BLESSINGS*

Let's celebrate our Country's birthday
A Happy Fourth of July.
Let's ring the bells of Freedom
Wave the flag against the sky.

Let's remember how great the cost
Of Freedom's glorious light.
Let it shine deep within our hearts
And keep it burning bright.

Let's remember those who shed their blood
On fields of battle, through the years.
They kept our Flag waving high
With dedication, blood, and tears.

We think of places light Arlington
Where brave young heroes rest.
In their homeland they loved so much
And for it, they gave their best.

So, let's have our parades — and sing our songs.
And watch "Old Glory" go by
As veterans from all past wars march
It brings a tear to our eye.

So let us say a prayer of thanks
That we live in this beautiful land
For Patriot's dreams, and courage
And blessings, from God's loving hand.

# WE THANK THEE

Let us be thankful
Our blessings have been good.
And let us not forget
To thank and praise our Lord.

Let us thank Him for our freedom
And that we live in this great land.
Where we can choose to worship Good
And we know He will understand.

Let us thank Him for the bounty
For our fields of ripened grain
And for the trees, heavy with fruit
That we will be fed, once again.

Let us thank Him for love
Of family and friends, so dear.
And also for our homes
That shelter us year after year.

But most of all we thank Him
For the great love he has shown.
How he sent His Son to save us
And we are not His own.

So let us count our blessings
And at the end of each day
Let us never forget to thank Him
As we kneel down to pray.

# *A MODERN THANKSGIVING*

Thanksgiving Day is not the same
As it was forty years ago.
We went to Grandma and Grandpa's house
Through the woods, and in the snow.

Now, Grandma and Grandpa has sold the Place
And moved into a condominium.
There isn't room for all of us
And all the pandemonium.

And sometimes they are packed up
In their brand new mobile home
They headed for the warm sunshine
Where they can be alone.

We make lots of telephone calls
Across the miles, so far away.
While the turkey roasts in the oven
And the children are at play.

I guess we will make our own traditions
Our children will come home to us
We will meet around the table
To enjoy our Thanksgiving feast.

But, somehow we will be united
As we bow our heads to pray
Our family love will bind us
On this Thanksgiving Day.

# NO ROOM IN THE INN

There was no room in the inn
For Mary and Joseph that night.
They were tired and weary, from travel,
Only God knew of their plight.

The inn was crowded
People rushing to and fro
The innkeeper didn't realize
Whom he had turned away from his door.

How could he know that God's Son
Was entering this world here below.
That on this night of miracles
Your love would over flow.

No room in the inn, they said
But we have a warm stable, that will do
And there with the animals and in a manger
God's Son was born for me and you.

Love came down to earth, that night
And your glory shown all around.
The shepherds saw your Angels
No greater love can be found.

Peace on earth, the Angels say
Do not be afraid they said
They saw the Star over Bethlehem.
And by it's light — they were led.

When we close our hears to Jesus
No room in there, we say.
We are like that innkeeper, of old
We put our Lord away.

Let us all take this time
And worship that Baby, God's Son.
Let us take Him out of the stable
And make room — in our hearts, for Him.

# CHRISTMAS REMEMBRANCE

It's Christmas once again
And everything is going fine.
The tree is up—the cards sent
And all done—just in time.

So, now I sit and think
About times so long ago
Those happy faces smiling
With Christmas love aglow.

It seems I hear laughter
And those voices some now stilled.
We were making happy memories
Our hearts with love were filled.

We gathered around the Christmas tree
With gifts stacked to the top.
There were presents there for everyone
For weeks we all did shop.

There was food for all to eat
Turkey, Pie and Cake.
Prepared with loving hands so dear
There was nothing we didn't make.

I sit here in the twilight
The Christmas lights all-aglow
My memory takes me back again
To that wonderful time long ago.

It's time to put those thoughts away
The preset time calls for me
But somewhere inside my heart
Those thoughts will stay with me.

Oh—look—thought my window
I see the brightest star
And, I wonder about that other one
That brought men from afar.

It's light shone round about
Never before such love was given
That little baby came to earth
To light our way to Heaven.

# *HEAVENLY STAR*

Suddenly, there was a Star
It appeared in the Heavens that night.
The shepherds saw it first
And was filled with a terrible fright.

It seemed to shine upon the earth
With such a glow and light.
They wondered what it could be
Oh, what a beautiful sight.

So, there appeared the Angels
Telling them not to be afraid
That they had good news for them
About a baby, who in a manger, laid.

Peace on earth they sang
Praises to the New Born King.
God's Son has come to earth today
Hear the Angels sing.

The shepherds said, "Let us go,
And see this wondrous thing
The Star will guide us to Him
To Christ, the New Born King."

And as they looked in wonder
There beneath the Star He lay
It seemed to shine down from Heaven
A Baby — in a manger of hay.

The light shone all around
It's beams in the sky, was not lost.
Behold, the rays touched His head
For a moment-it formed a Cross.

# LIGHTS OF CHRISTMAS

There were shepherds on the hill
Watching their flocks by night
When suddenly the angels sang
And there was a Heavenly light.

The light shone all around
And filled their hearts with fear.
But they said, "Be not afraid
We bring tidings of cheer."

For that night, a baby was born
And brought to the world, great joy
There in a manger he lay
A beautiful boy.

Because you see, there was no room
In the Inn that night, for them.
I'm sure that God led them there
To the stable in Bethlehem.

And there God's Son was born
On that night, so long ago.
A Star appeared in the Heavens
And made the whole world glow.

An innocent, beautiful little baby
He came to save us from sit.
He will lead us, into God's presence
If we will let him, enter in.

So let us light our lights
And decorate our Christmas tree
To let the whole world know
That Christ lives, in you and me.

# *LET THE BELLS RING*

Happy New Year — Let the bells ring
The eighties are history
Let's welcome the nineties with faith
We hope they bring peace, to you and me.

We are going into the last decade
Of the twentieth century
We have seen so many things happen
There is so much yet to be.

This New Year is special
It's a gateway for better things.
And when we reach the year two thousand
We will be ready for what it brings.

We know that God is with us
And that He is always there.
Let's ask His blessing on us
All through the coming year!

Happy New Year!

# CHAPTER SEVEN

# JESUS - THE MAN

# BE PREPARED

If Jesus came to your house
To have a visit with you
Would you be ready, and welcome Him
Just what would you do?

Could you find your Bible
To put in a closer place?
Would you hurry and dust it off
With a welcome smile on your face?

Could you open your door
And reach out your hands to Him?
And nor worry about what He would see
When He stepped within?

Would He see the love inside?
Would He feel God's Spirit there?
Would you care for Him to see
The open book, beside your chair?

What about the T.V.?
Would you invite Him in to share?
One of your favorite shows you love?
Or would you be ashamed, with Him there?

So, the best thing we can do
Is prepare for Him to come.
Chang our lives, and do His will
And wait, and welcome — God's Holy Son.

# THE BEAUTIFUL HANDS OF JESUS

How beautiful are the hands of Jesus
As He used them when He walked among Men?
How He drew little children to Him
And He showed His great love for them.

With loving hands He fed the five thousand
From a lunch of a youngster in the crowd.
He blessed the five loaves and two fishes
And there was more than enough to go around.

There was the time on the storm tossed sea
His disciples were filled with fear.
He raised His hands upward to Heaven
The waves were calmed, and the sky was clear.

He must have raised His hands to God
When He called Lazarus from the dead.
How His heart ached for Mary and Martha
As He wept with them, His tears were shed.

When they met in the upper room together
For the Passover feast to share
How He took His hands and broke the bread
And passed the cup to them there.

One time He washed His disciple's feet
Because He loved them, you see.
The hands of the Master cleansed them
To show humility to you and me.

And after His resurrection
The disciples had fished all night.
Jesus had cooked and served them breakfast
To them He was a beautiful sight.

Oh, wouldn't you have loved to have been there?
As Jesus walked among men
Just to have reached out, and touched those hands
How wonderful it would have been.

Now Jesus has gone from this earth
To prepare for us a place in Heaven
His nailed scarred hands are guiding us Home
Because His life for us was given.

Oh, how beautiful are the hands of Jesus
I'll say it again and again.
He is still reaching out to us — to come
And have eternal life with Him.

# *WHO IS THIS MAN?*

Who is this Man
Who walked here years ago?
He came to bring us love
To this old world below.

He left His home in Heaven
Because, it was the only way.
He was the last sacrifice
His blood washed us clean, that day.

As He walked here
He saw the suffering and pain.
And with His loving touch
He made them whole again.

He cleansed the Lepers.
He made the blind to see.
He healed the lame and helpless
As He walked with them, making them free.

He fed the hungry multitude
As they followed Him that day.
A little boy's loaves and fishes
Took their hunger away.

He loved the little children
And said, "Let them come unto Me"
He gathered them close, around Him
As He drew them to His knee.

He calmed the raging storm
As they crossed the lake that day.
The winds and waves, heard His voice
And they were safe, the rest of the way.

He cast out evil spirits.
He turned the water into wine.
He walked upon the water
He was God's Son — divine.

Who is this Man?
He carried a Cross—to Calvary.
He suffered, and bled, and died
That we might live—eternally.

His name was Jesus.
He lives now, in Heaven above.
He is watching, and waiting, for us there
Where we will abide, forever, in His Love.

Who is the Man? HE IS LORD!

# HE CAME IN LOVE

There were three crosses on a hill
Where our Savior bled and died.
He walked up the hill to Calvary
And there, was crucified.

He was a man who came in love
With a kiss He was betrayed.
For thirty pieces of silver
The terrible deed was made.

He was shamed and humiliated.
A crown of thorns was placed on His head.
He stood alone before Pilate
All of His friends had fled.

He heard the crowd cry, "CRUCIFY!"
When there was a chance to go free
He had to fulfill the prophecy
That He would die for you and me.

He hung suspended on that cross
He asked His Father to forgive.
For this reason He came to earth
That all of might live.

But early Sunday morning
He arose from the dead!
The angels rolled the stone away
It happened — just as He said.

He is Risen — He is Risen!
The whole world sings this song.
We rejoice — because He Lives
And we praise Him all day long.

This man who came in love
He did His Father's will.
He now lives in Heaven
And He is loving us still.

# NO GREATER LOVE

He was alone, standing there
He was brought before Pilate, ruler over all
The Roman Governor, who found not fault
With the innocent Man — there in his hall.

Pilate had the power to release Jesus.
The Lamb — God's only Son.
The chief priests, and the leaders, full of hate
Each accused Him, one by one.

As the mob cried, "Crucify Him"
Pilate finally gave up, and washed his hands
Saying, "I am innocent now,
Of the blood, of this good Man."

So, the Roman soldiers took Him away.
They placed a crown of thorns upon His head.
A purple robe was put on Him
To this painful death — he was led.

Then they took a wooded cross
To carry up to Calvary.
He fell beneath the heavy load
Carrying the sins — of you and me.

He washed away our sins
As His precious blood flowed — that day.
He said, "Forgive them Father, they know not what they do" As his life, drained away.

But death could not hold Him
Because He was God's precious Son.
On the third day, He arose, and left the tomb
And forever changed the world — for everyone.

He bled and died upon that cross
A sacrifice for you and me.
Let's always remember His great love
That gave to us — Eternity!

# LITTLE LOST LAMB

I am just a little lamb
You see I'm not very old.
I wandered far away from Home
Away from the sheltering fold.

My Mama told me not to go.
But the shining lights were so bright.
I disobeyed, and lost my way
Out into the cold dark night.

So now, I'm cold and hungry
All I can do is weep.
I'm looking for my Shepherd
And all the other sheep.

I wish I hadn't strayed away
I need your loving care.
Won't you help me find my Shepherd
He is looking for me somewhere?

He always comes to find us
When we have lost our way.
He lifts us in His loving arms
And takes us Home to stay.

# THE GOOD SHEPHERD

There is a little lamb, that strayed away
From the safety of the fold.
We ask the Good Shepherd to go and find
And lift him out of the cold.

It's so dark, and so cold.
The path is steep and drear.
The bushes and brambles, are all around
He trembles now with fear.

He left the others from the fold
As he looked across the way
To the bright lights, and loud music
And the crowds that are at play.

It all looked so enticing
With laughter all around.
So somehow, he strayed too far
And got lost in all the sound.

Satan is always looking
For the ones, who are straying away.
His is a sly old fox — just waiting
For a brother to loose his way.

But the Good Shepherd is always looking
And watching everyday.
He sees His little lamb straying
And He is reaching out, to pray.

So little lamb, don't go so far
The night is falling fast.
Reach out to the Shepherd passing by
He will find you at last.

We know that the Shepherd is the Lord
And we are His sheep, that He loves.
He wants us safely gathered in
To His Heavenly Fold above.

# GOD'S POINTS OF LIGHT

Help me to be a point of light
In this old world today.
Darkness has fallen upon us
We need to light our way.

The shadows seem to fall
Sometimes, it only take a smile.
To lift the shadows, from someone's heart
To make their life worth while.

There is always someone
That needs a helping hand.
If we would look around us
All over this great land.

So let us light a candle
In our corner of our place.
And pray we can touch a life
And put a smile on their face.

It could be in a market place
We may see a friend in despair.
Let us take the time to reach out
And show them that we care.

God has given us the light.
If we would only let it shine.
He wants us to be beacons
Showing his love divine.

So, we can all be points of light
Like a glowing star from above.
We know God's hand will lead us
As He lights us, with His love.

# GIFTS OF LIGHT

God knew we couldn't live in darkness.
He said, "Let there be light."
So He gave us the sun by day
And the moon and the stars by night.

Light is one of the most precious gifts
The world has ever known.
Everyday has a point of light
Through which God's love is shown.

Sometimes when we are down
We need something to come to our sight.
Suddenly, a flash of cardinal's wing
And there it is — the gift of light.

If we only look everyday
We can find your point of light.
Sometimes it is in the morning star
That takes away the dark of night.

It may be a bouquet of dandelions
Picked by a child's little hand.
It was brought in, from your own backyard
Nothing else could be so grand.

Everyday there will be a gift of light
That unexpected we will find.
Tucked away, in a drawer or closet
It brings sweet memories to our mind.

God gives us light in many ways
In His word you will find
His message lights up our lives each day
And opens up the windows of our mind.

So, light the light in you heart each day
In everything you do.
Reach out, and touch someone in need
And love will come back to you!

# PRAYERS AND THANKSGIVING

I said a prayer today
My heart was full of love.
It was a prayer of Thanksgiving
For blessings from above.

I thanked Him for his guidance
And how He cared for me.
How He carried me through the shadows
And from sit He set me free.

I know I am so unworthy
But He has given me eternal life.
He sent His Son to save me
He made me see the light.

So, I'll sing His praises daily
My prayer I know He hears.
I'll thank Him for His blessings
And how He calms my fears.

Yes, I said a prayer today
To than Him for His love
Because He watches over me
From His heavenly home above.

# FRIENDS

Do you have a friend
To walk with you each day?
One to share your sunshine
And shadows along the way?

A friends is one of God's sweetest gifts
He knew we would need someone to care
When storms appear on the horizon
That friend is always there.

When we are very happy
And things are going fine
We need a friend to laugh with us
And share our warm sunshine.

I have a friend who walks with me
Through the hills and valleys of life.
He is with me in the darkness
And also in the light.

His name is Jesus
And you can have Him too.
He is our Lord and Savior
Sent from Heaven for me and you.

# CHAPTER EIGHT

---

# THE UNITED STATES OF AMERICA

# AMERICA OUR HOME

We live in a land called America.
The home of the brave and the free.
We enjoy the freedoms that we have
Made of you and me.

For our freedoms, we paid a high price.
Is cost us, in toil, blood and tears.
So we could have a firm foundation
For our country down through the years.

God is America's foundation
The cornerstone in our homes, and families, so true.
They called God, "The Divine Hand of Providence".
And families were people like me and you.

The Flag is our symbol of loyalty
The Stars and Stripes, flying high.
We are so proud, when se see her there
Waving against the blue sky.

So, let be thankful for our homeland
Let us count our blessings today
That we live in this Country called America
The good old USA!

# *WE THE PEOPLE*

We the people of this land
Have been so blessed by God above.
The Divine Hand of Providence
Guided our ancestors, in love.

Our country was found long ago
They had a very wonderful plan.
That we are all created equal
And Freedom, came into the heart of man.

Freedom was the reason
They paid the price of Glory.
To worship God, the way they chose
Was the important part of our story.

We are the people of our Homeland
We have always answered, when duty called.
We always had those, who gave their best
They left everything and gave their all.

We built churches, and schools, to educate.
We farmed the land, with animals and grain.
Our homes were built on a solid foundation
To seek the rainbow after the rain.

God gave us beautiful Limestone
That is well known everywhere
The people here quarried the rock
And made it possible for the world to share.

In this area, we came together.
We the people, heart to heart, and hand in hand
Always trying for a better tomorrow.
Guided along-by God's own hand.

       WE THE PEOPLE……..

# OUR FLAG

I love to see "Old Glory" wave
Against a clear blue sky.
It makes me feel so wonderful
Watching her there so high.

I think of what it stands for
And how precious it is to us all.
And how much it has meant to America
And to the ones, who wouldn't let her fall.

There has been so much bloodshed
To keep it flying free.
So much love for our Country
Made safe for you and me.

So, when you see that flag
Flying in the breeze, so fair
 Pledge allegiance in your heart
And thank God, it's still there.

Let's keep those colors up there
Flying high where all may see.
Everyone will know we love our Country
The Home and the Brave and the Free.

# *A DAY OF INFAMY*

On a beautiful day in September
Shining in the Golden Sun
The Twin Towers in New York City
Was a beacon to all who would come.

It was business as usual, that morning
People hurrying to and fro
Rushing to their destinations
To where they did not know.

How could they know that Evil
Had a date with destiny that day.
Bringing death and destruction to many
As they rushed, innocently, on their way.

Two planes, full speed ahead
Hit the Towers and the nightmare had begun.
Soon black smoke and debris filled the air
So bad it blotted out the sun.

Firemen and Police came quickly
They saw dear friends die that day.
So many left home that morning became heroes
Trying to get people out of harm's way.

For days the darkness was there
Rescuing victims and saving lives
Help came from all over America
Bringing Doctors and Nurses and medical supplies.

The Governor and Mayor were there every day
With broken hearts they looked on the scene
Signs of death were everywhere
It seemed they were walking in a dream.

Though Evil had come that day
God's love was everywhere.
Out of the ruins, a cross was found
As a Memorial for all to share.

It's been a year, since it happened
NINE ONE ONE — will echo across the land.
No one will ever be the same again
As we all will lend our hearts and hands.

Again blue skies are over Ground Zero
Flags are waving beautiful and free.
The Twin Towers are gone forever
And God is still watching over you and me!

# MIRACLE OF GROUND ZERO

In those days of darkness
After the Towers came down
They were searching through the debris
To see if anyone could be found.

The City was hurting in sorrow and grief
As Search and Rescue workers were called in
They knew survivors might still be there
Even though there were no signs of life heard or seen.

An Excavation laborer answered the call
A native of the City he loved.
He wasn't prepared for what he would see
But he would be led by God above.

By this time all who were working
Day and night in the debris
Were so tired and burdened by grief
Driven by a force unknown to you and me.

Into the depths of Hell they went
Masked, and a wet bandana to cover the nose
Into a choking stench and a blanket of dust
And a deadly silence, no cries arose.

After twelve hours of searching they couldn't quit
And this man decided to "look over there"
It was once the lobby atrium that had become a grotto
The pale light of dawn, shone down on, shapes to share.

What is this — How did they get here?
Crosses, the largest one was twenty feet high.
There were other smaller crosses around
Where I fell to my knees and cried!

I felt I could hear God saying
"This was done in evil — but I will turn it for good."
As we all came there, fell to their knees, crying,
Some singing, some praying, in this hallowed space.

There was no doubt that God was there
And I felt that Jesus wept again.
As everyone was changed by that cross
A message of Hope no one could explain.

Finally, they tore away the ruins there
And Father Jordan persuaded them to save the cross
Workers mounted it on a forty foot foundation
So workers in the Pit could see it by looking up.

New life will rise from the ashes
I know, because that cross was a sign of Love.
A promise from God — that He is with us
Keeping watch from Heaven above!

    It truly was a Miracle

# CHAPTER NINE

# DESERT STORM

# RIBBONS FOR REMEMBRANCE

There are lots of yellow ribbons
Appearing every day.
It's our way to honor those
Who are so far away.

They left their homes and families
It was so hard for them to do.
But they knew it was their job
To make the world safe, for me and you.

So let us keep them in our hearts.
Let them know we really care.
Sent them letters, cards and anything
That will make life easier to bear.

There's one thing we can do
To show them, we want to share
Tie those yellow ribbons on everything
Keep them flying in the air.

We will put them on our doors
And tie them around every tree.
We will decorate our cars
Until everyone is free.

When we tie a yellow ribbon
It will be from heart to hearts
One end is tied to theirs
And the other one around ours.

So, let us keep them in our prayers
And ask God to bless them in every way.
Give them strength, and keep them safe
Until they come home, someday.

# DESERT STORM

There is a storm blowing
Across the deserts sands.
There is a great army gathered there
Coming from every land.

Our troops are waiting there
And they know the time will come.
The call will come for service
And we pray for them — everyone.

They came from all walks of life.
They left it all behind
To keep our Freedom safe
For the good of all mankind.

We want them to know-their Country
Loves them, each and every one.
We wave our flags, tie yellow ribbons
Until the last one will come home.

So, day and night-we pray and ask
God to protect them all the way
And bring them back to their families
Once again to stay.

Yes, there is a desert storm blowing
Across the desert sands
Only God, can calm the winds
And bring PEACE to the lands.

May it be soon.

# PEACE AFTER THE STORM

The Desert Storm is over
The winds of war have ceased.
The thunder has stopped rolling
At last — we have Peace.

Now, we are looking for the rainbow
As the clouds roll away.
The sun is coming out
For a brand new day.

The line in the desert sand
Is no longer there.
It's been swept away, by our armed forces
And each one doing their share.

Once again, Freedom will ring
As peace comes to the land.
Liberation is felt among the people
Everyone lending a hand.

Our troops will be coming home
To those they hold so dear.
Love will be everywhere
Our hearts will no longer fear.

Let us never take for granted
How much our Freedom means.
To have the right to live
And work toward our dreams.

Truly, America is beautiful
We want to say thanks today.
To our brave sons and daughters
Who will always, keep Her that way.

So, the Desert Storm is over
We ask God to heal the land.
And God Bless America
And the truths, for which she stands.

# WHEELS ACROSS THE DESERT

The wheels are rolling
Across the desert sand.
Bringing them back toward home
To leave that dreary land.

The war is over now
Our troops are homeward bound.
The large convoys are moving
Leaving their trails behind.

We welcome our heroes home
Back to the ones they love.
All of them smiling through tears
Everyone thankful, to God above.

In time the tracks in the desert
Will be covered, and gone.
The winds will shift the sands
The footprints will have blown.

But to those who were there
Memories will be in their hearts.
The heat, the cold, the fire and rain
From their minds — will never depart.

They will never forget those faces
Their hunger, pain and fears.
The children needing shelter
It never changes, through the years.

As in all wars
So many things are left undone.
But we must leave it in God's hands
And meet the rising sun.

So, let us be glad and welcome
Our troops all back, today.
Let us let them know, we love them
And pray — they are home to stay!

We Thank Our God —

# ABOUT THE AUTHOR

Jewell Gill was born in Smithville, Indiana on December 13, 1914 to Robert and Permelia Gill.

She married Harry Meadows in 1937 and they had two children. She was widowed in 1944 through a tragic accident and was left to raise two small children.

She lived in Smithville until she married Charles Libkie in 1952 and then moved to Ellettsville, Indiana.

Throughout her life she has had a strong faith and has tried to live her life according to the New Testament. She started writing poetry sometime in her mid-60s. Her family teased her about being the "Grandma Moses of Poetry". She has written poems to celebrate the birthdays, weddings and anniversaries of her friends and family.

1 Peter 4:10 "Each one should use whatever gift he has received to serve others, faithfully administering God's grace in various forms."

Printed in the United States
26490LVS00005B/364-381